SHARE YOUR
BEST WISHES HERE!
I0797745

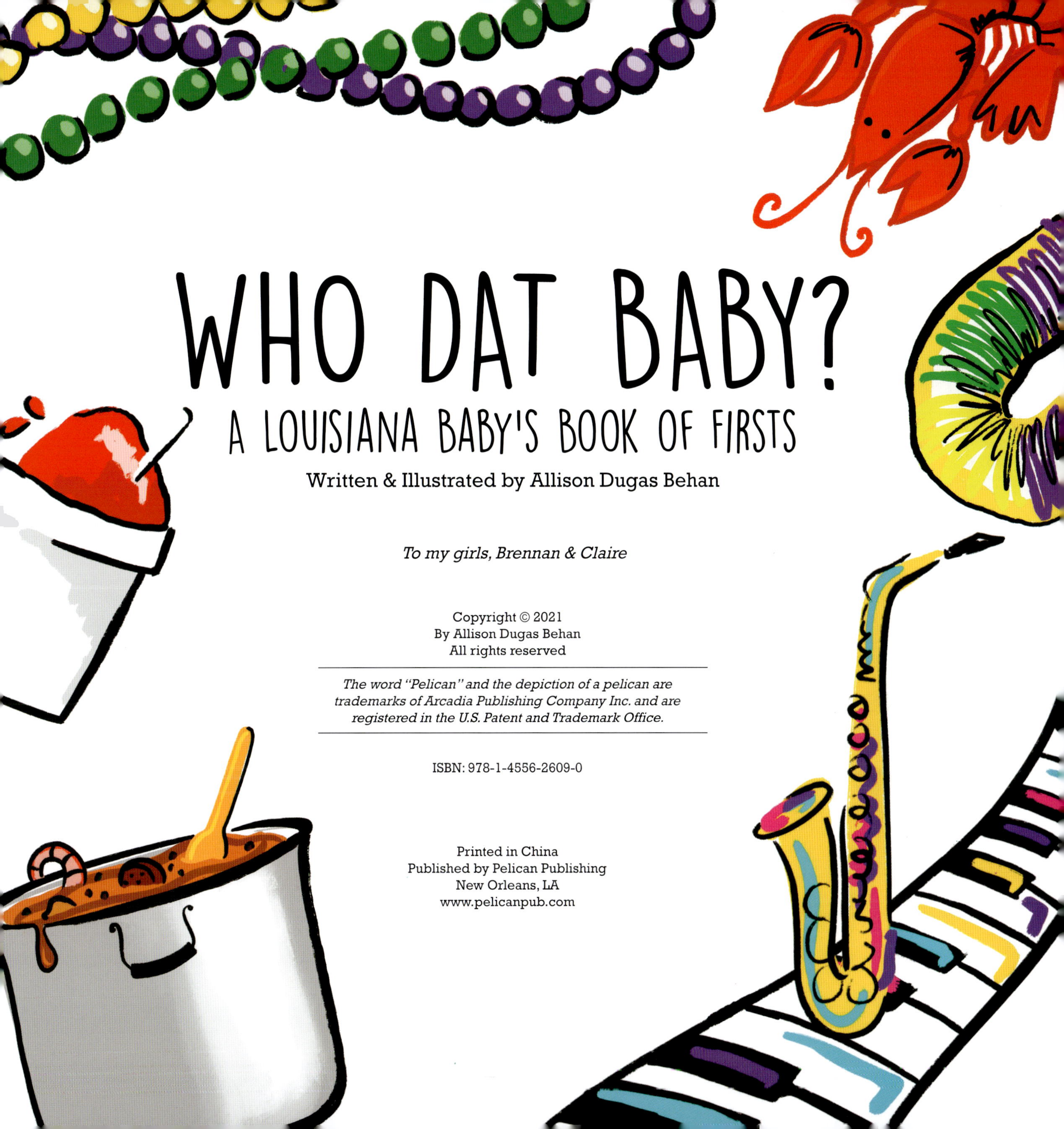

WHO DAT BABY?

A LOUISIANA BABY'S BOOK OF FIRSTS

Written & Illustrated by Allison Dugas Behan

To my girls, Brennan & Claire

ISBN: 978-1-4556-2609-0

Printed in China
Published by Pelican Publishing
New Orleans, LA
www.pelicanpub.com

BIENVENUE

NAME

BIRTHDAY

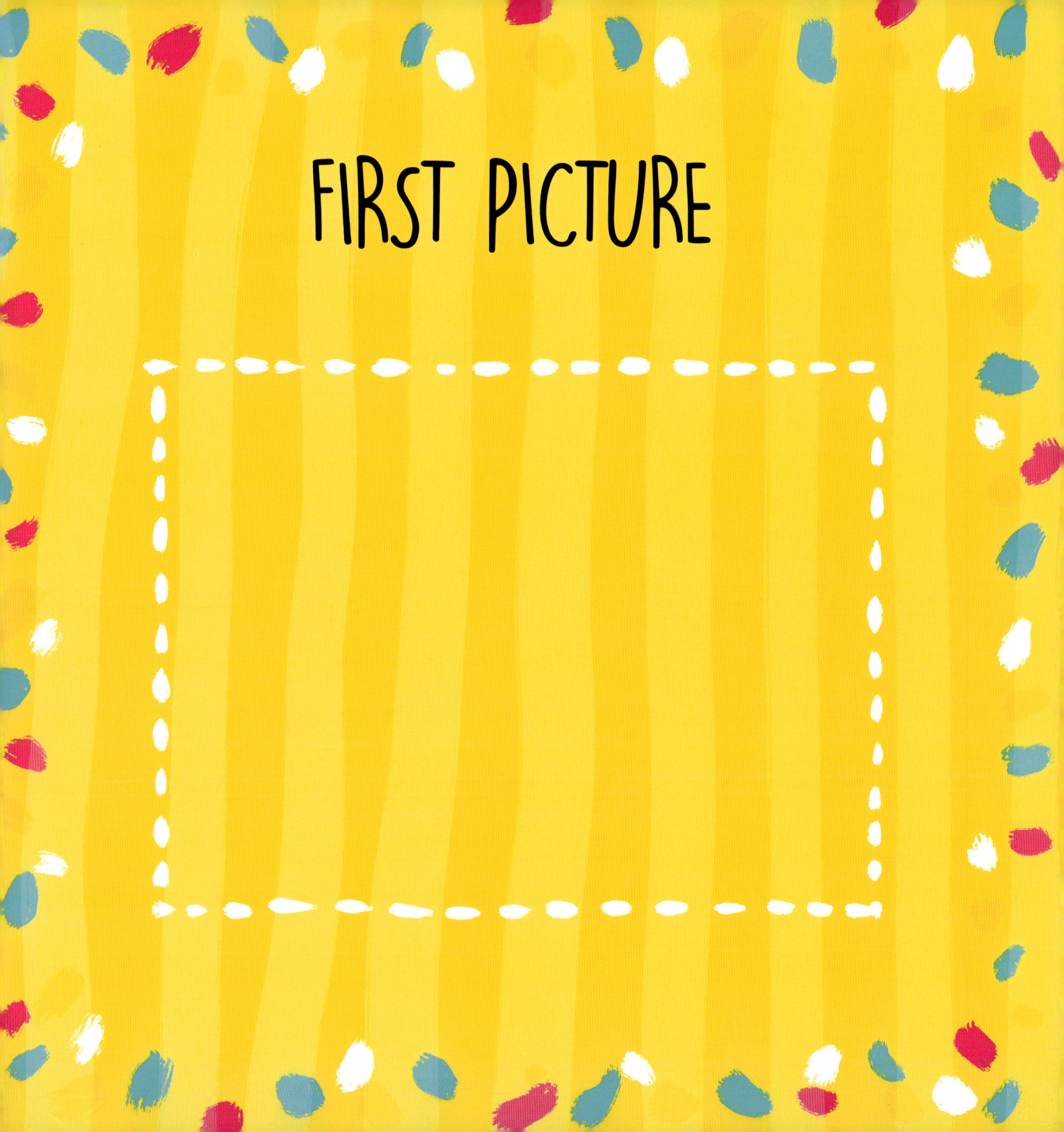
FIRST PICTURE

FAMILY
WHO'S YA MAMA AN DEM?

FOOTPRINTS
HANDPRINTS

MY FAMILY

WHO DAT

TIME

DATE

WEIGHT

HOSPITAL

LENGTH

WHERE Y'AT?

MY FIRST ADDRESS

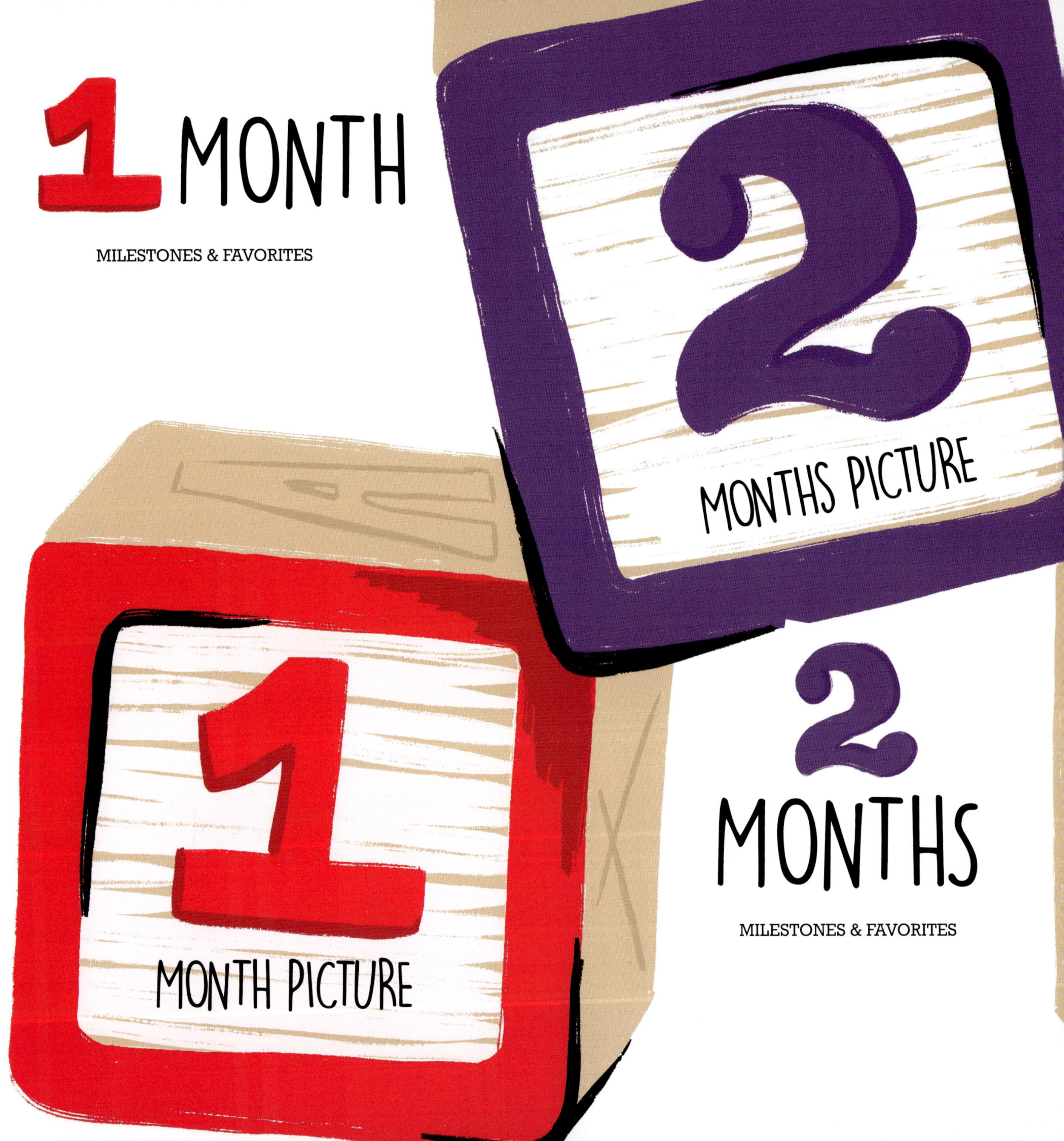
1 MONTH
MILESTONES & FAVORITES
2
MONTHS PICTURE
1
MONTH PICTURE
2
MONTHS
MILESTONES & FAVORITES

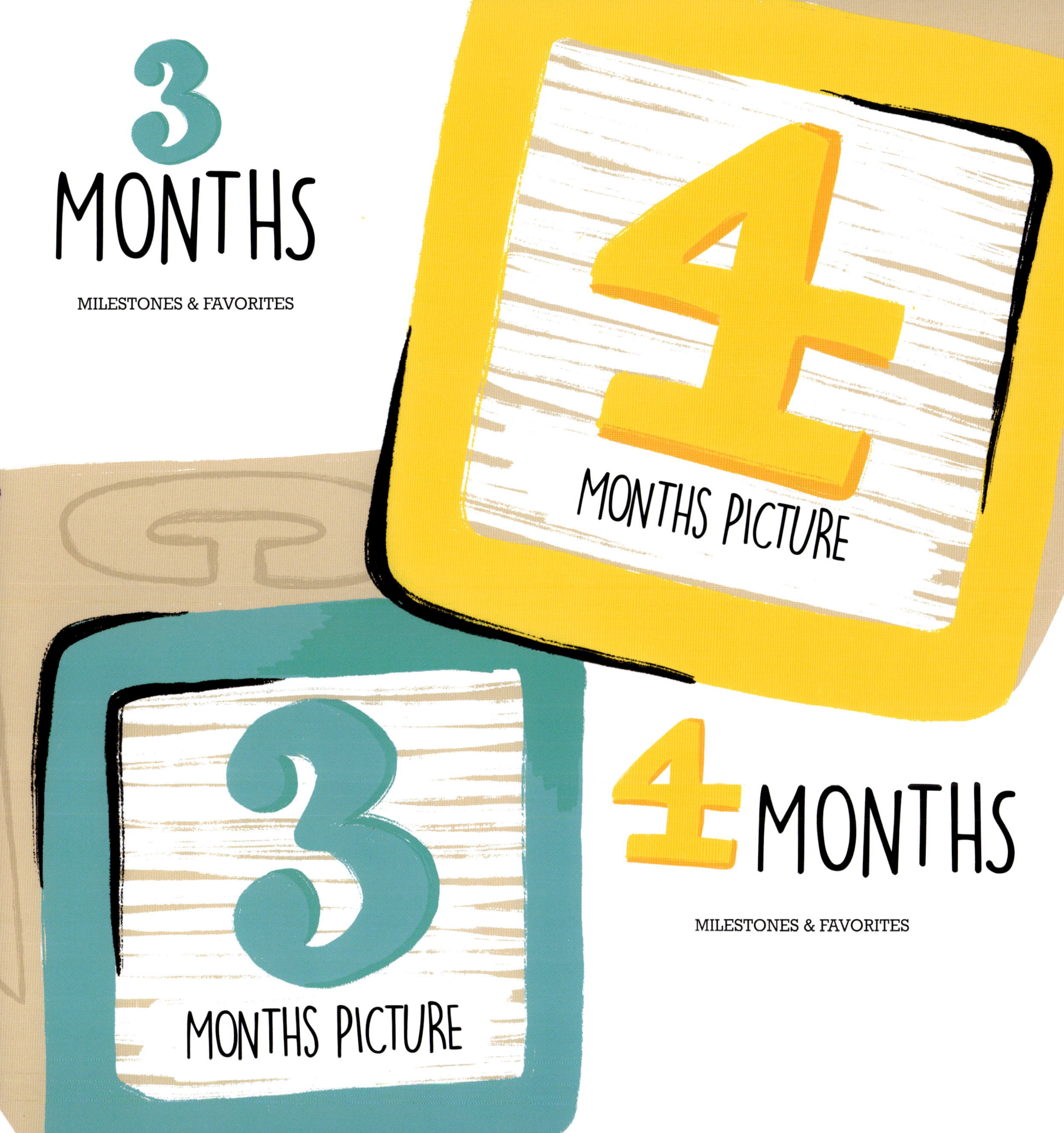
3
MONTHS
MILESTONES & FAVORITES
4
MONTHS PICTURE
3
MONTHS PICTURE
4 MONTHS
MILESTONES & FAVORITES

5
MONTHS PICTURE
6
MONTHS
MILESTONES & FAVORITES
5 MONTHS
MILESTONES & FAVORITES
6
MONTHS PICTURE

7
MONTHS PICTURE
8 MONTHS
MILESTONES & FAVORITES
7
MONTHS
MILESTONES & FAVORITES
8
MONTHS PICTURE

9 MONTHS

MILESTONES & FAVORITES

10 MONTHS

MILESTONES & FAVORITES

MILESTONES & FAVORITES

12
MONTHS PICTURE

11
MONTHS PICTURE

12 MONTHS

MILESTONES & FAVORITES

PARTY THEME
PARTY LOCATION
SPECIAL GUESTS
FAVORITE GIFTS
1
1ST BIRTHDAY

2ND BIRTHDAY
PARTY THEME
SPECIAL GUESTS
PARTY LOCATION
FAVORITE GIFTS

MAKIN'

GROCERIES

FIRST BEIGNET

DATE

CAFÉ

WHO TOOK ME

FIRST RED BEANS AND RICE

DATE

WHO MADE 'EM

MY REACTION

FIRST SNOBALL

DATE

FLAVOR

STAND

FIRST PRALINE

DATE

BAKERY

FIRST KING CAKE
I GOT THE BABY!
DATE
FLAVOR
BAKERY

FIRST CRAWFISH
DATE
PLACE
MY REACTION

FIRST GUMBO

LAISSEZ LES BONS

TEMPS ROULER

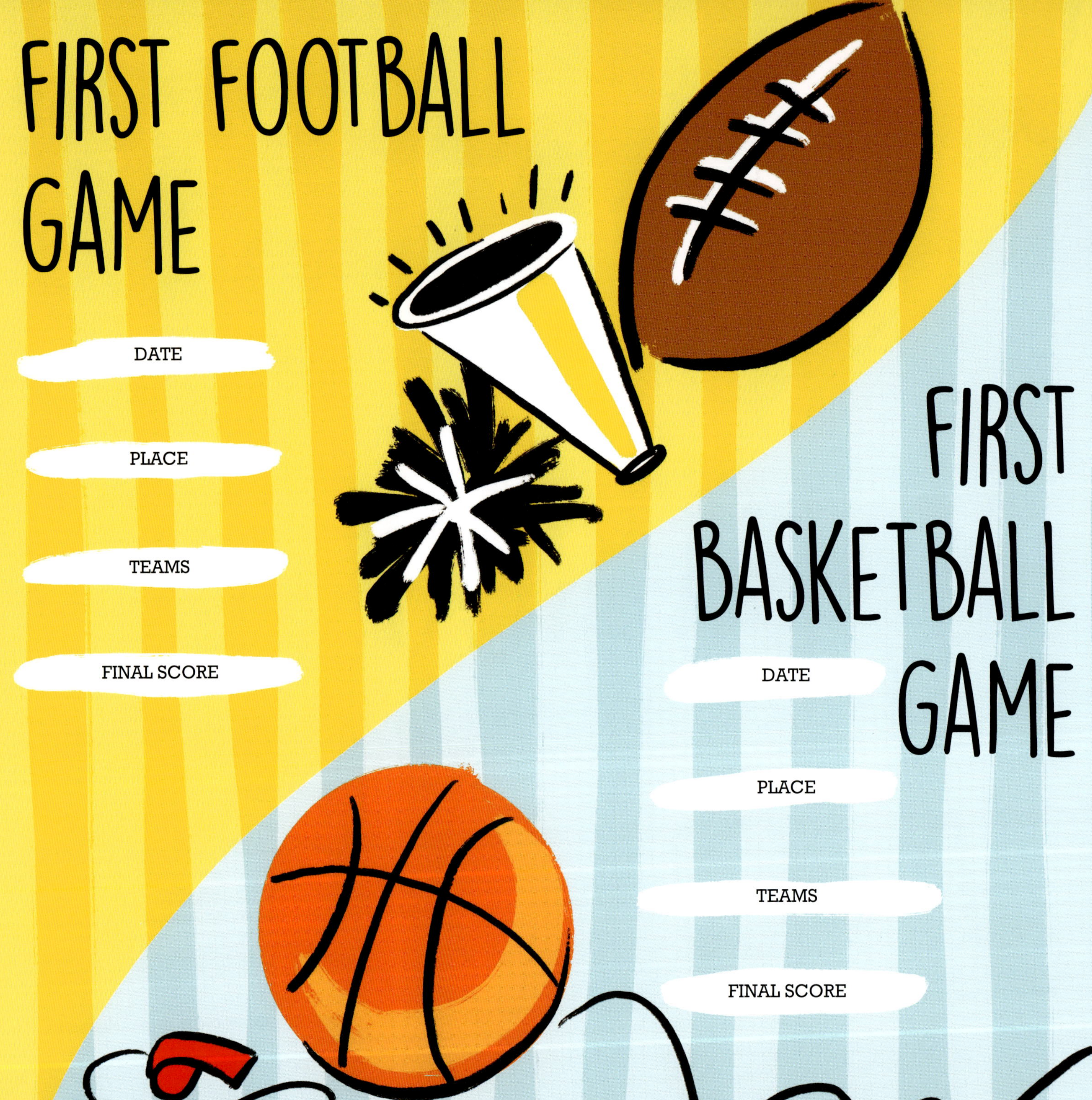
FIRST FOOTBALL GAME
DATE
PLACE
TEAMS
FINAL SCORE
FIRST BASKETBALL GAME
DATE
PLACE
TEAMS
FINAL SCORE

FIRST PARADE

FIRST
SWAMP TOUR
DATE
PLACE
FAVORITE SIGHTS
PEOPLE WITH ME

FIRST FESTIVAL
DATE
FESTIVAL NAME
WHO WENT WITH ME
WHAT I ENJOYED

FIRST ZOO TRIP

FIRST AQUARIUM TRIP

DATE

AQUARIUM NAME

WHO WENT WITH ME

FAVORITE ANIMAL

FIRST MUSEUM
DATE
MUSEUM NAME
FAVORITE EXHIBIT
PEOPLE WITH ME

FIRST VISIT TO THE FRENCH QUARTER
DATE
PLACES I EXPLORED
THINGS I ATE
PEOPLE WITH ME

FIRST FISHING TRIP
DATE
WHO TOOK ME
LOCATION
WHAT I CAUGHT

FIRST FAIS DO-DO

DATE

PLACE

WHO WENT WITH ME

FAVORITE DANCE

FIRST BOAT RIDE

DATE

NAME OF BOAT

FAVORITE SIGHTS

PEOPLE WITH ME

FIRST FAIS DO-DO

DATE

PLACE

WHO WENT WITH ME

FAVORITE DANCE

FIRST BOAT RIDE

DATE

NAME OF BOAT

FAVORITE SIGHTS

PEOPLE WITH ME

FIRST STREETCAR RIDE
DATE
LINE
DESTINATION

A LITTLE LAGNIAPPE

FIRST SMILE
DATE

FIRST LAUGH
DATE

FIRST ROLL OVER
DATE

FIRST CRAWL
DATE

FIRST TIME SITTING UP
DATE

FIRST STEPS
DATE

FIRST TIME I WALKED
DATE

FIRST WORD
DATE

FAVORITE SONG

FAVORITE FOOD

FAVORITE TV SHOW

FAVORITE TOY

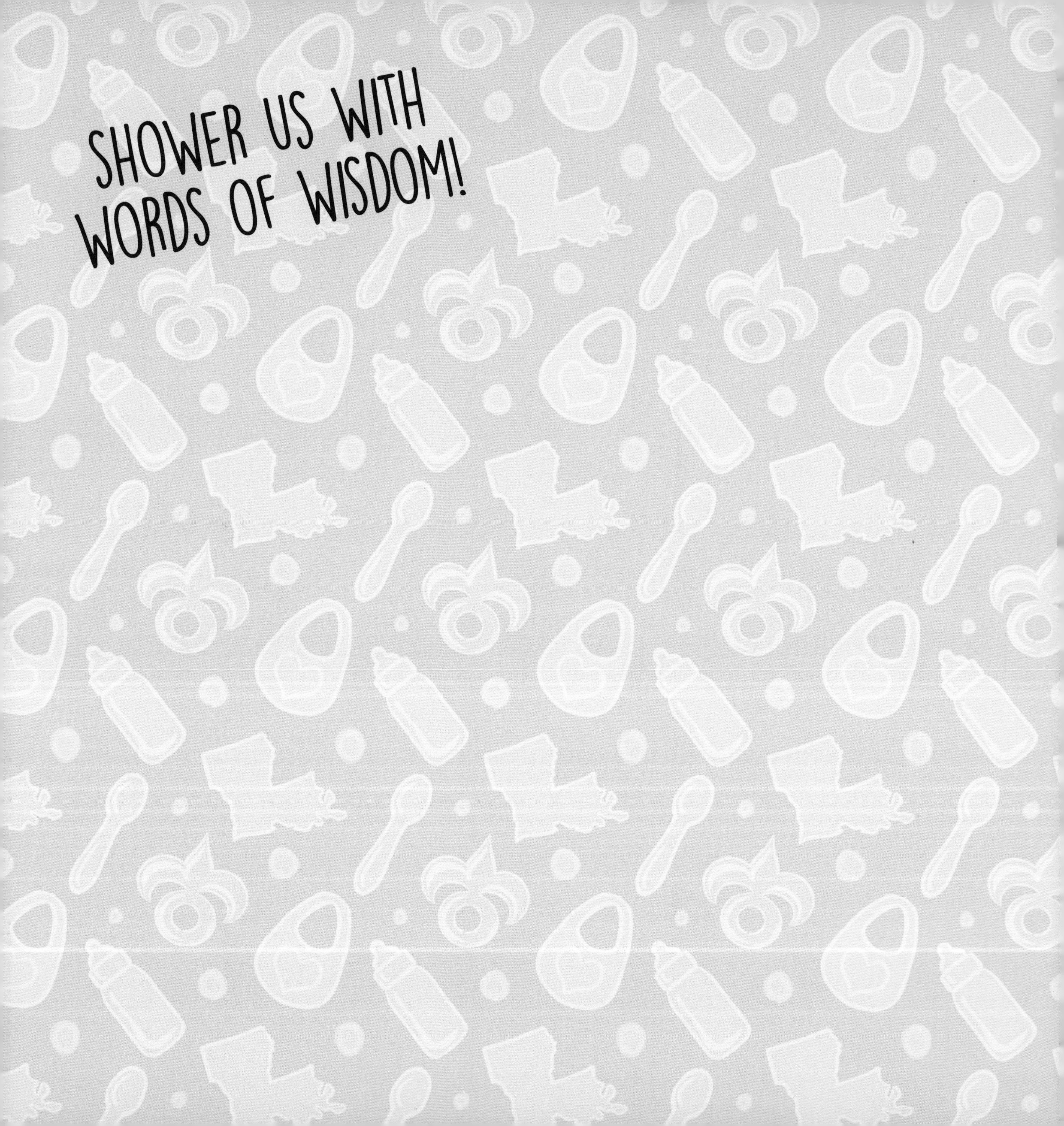
SHOWER US WITH
WORDS OF WISDOM!